Legacy Building

Through Extraordinary Leadership!

Judi;

My dearest friend in the Lord Jesus Christ! My Sister, My friend forever! I have the love of Jesus in my heart that "all is well" in your life beginning on this day! Love, Hugh 2018

Written by Hubert J. Littleton

The "Leadership Guru"

Copyright

Printed in the United States of America

First Printing, 2018

ISBN-13: 978-1-947656-51-2

ISBN10: 1947656511

The Butterfly Typeface Publishing
PO BOX 56193
Little Rock Arkansas 72215

www.butterflytypeface.com
butterflytypeface.imw@gmail.com

Dedication

This book is dedicated to the late Reverend and Mrs. Roosevelt and Margaret V. Littleton, my beloved Father and Mother.

My parents were married for over fifty-five years and raised three boys: Roosevelt Littleton, Jr., John A. Littleton, Hubert J. Littleton, (Hugh).

Their love, guidance and commitment to ensure that we achieve more in life than they did, proved to be the substance that enabled us to face all of life's adversities successfully.

In addition, they left me in the loving and protective arms of God, as now His child.

Preface

How I earned my Leadership PhD?

My parents instilled a level of accountability I could have never realized in any educational institution. Growing up in New Orleans, Louisiana the 17th Ward of Orleans Parish, I never knew I was poor. Yes, we were extremely poor! How poor were we? We were so poor that at one point in my life I recall living in a two-room house that was less than 200 square feet.

However, within those four walls was indescribable love! My mother cooked on a one burner electric hot plate. We all took baths in the same galvanized round tub my mother had previously washed our cloths.

In addition, our meals would sometimes consist of white flour bread with sugar sprinkled on top with a little tap water sprinkled over the sugared-bread, called "sugar water bread".

The upgrade to that meal was on special occasions we added butter to that "sugar water bread". The butter gave the bread and sugar a little more flavor. It was the best tasting meal I can remember. I often want to make sugar water bread just to remember and recapture the love my mother put in that meal I loved so much.

This all speaks to what my parents instilled in our minds, spirits and hearts to never forget where you came from and always make the best out of what some may say is a difficult situation. *For me, it was the best of times!*

What that now speaks to is a high level of emotional intelligence and accountability!

I grew up not knowing the business names, however, I clearly realize now in my adult life that because my parents never afforded us to think, feel, act, and/or look poor, it gave me a sense of emotional intelligence to face life's real-world experience with a greater sense of self-awareness, self-regulation, self-motivation, empathy and the ability to build effective relationships with anyone and everyone; at any given social and/or economic level.

In addition, the high-level of accountability enabled me to own my words, my actions and the process of my life experiences.

Additionally, my high-level of accountability afforded me the opportunity to understand that

I am responsible for everything that I say, do, and start!

You see with Accountability comes Responsibility and with Responsibility comes Accountability.

Accountability equates to "ownership" so, therefore I must own my words, own my actions, and frankly, own the process.

Accountability, means ownership!
It is doing what you say, and saying
what you mean. It is certainly, doing
the right-thing when no one is
looking. And, it is certainly doing the
right-thing when everyone is
looking! Accountability is just doing
the right-thing! It is the hardest
thing in life to do!

Table of Contents

Foreword

This book titled "Legacy Building Through Extraordinary Leadership" is the most inspiring book I have read! It is timely for the 21st Century of Leaders!

Hugh Littleton is delivering a strong and needed message to progressive leaders, who are facing a world of diversity. Hugh believes that diversity is no longer just sexual orientation, race, and/or social economics.

Hugh sees diversity as intellect! Leaders in today's progressive world are recognizing that employees, staff, peers are not just diverse with respect to the sexual orientation, race, and/or social economics, they are encountering progressive individuals with a high degree of intellect.

Intellect is the new defining yardstick that distinguishes performance from high performers. High performance now matters.

In the world of highly talented people, expectations are at its highest. The human capital is an investment for leaders. Leaders must understand that their priority is the investment in their people. Investment that will yield growth not only for the individual professionally, but for the enhancement and development of the organization at-large.

In addition, the powerful message of accountability is one for the ages. Hugh's message on accountability is one that leaders will embrace as an anchor for establishing a frame work for constructing a leadership legacy within any progressive organization.

In this book, Hugh is presenting tools, techniques, principles and methods to leaders who are committed, dedicated and focused on their people and the organization's advancement and sustainability.

Leaders with a clear and present desire to create a Legacy!

John A. Littleton

As a retired leader of a fortune 500 global organization, worked in one of the most prestigious organizations in the United States. I am honored to have an opportunity to share my thoughts regarding my brother Hubert J. Littleton and this amazing book.

Acknowledgement

My Big Brother John A. Littleton, is my inspiration for life! My brother John supported me throughout my life. As my worst critic, he also guided me through life's adversities in a tough love kind of way.

My most memorable moment is when I retired and he attended my extraordinary retirement celebration provided by my employer, one of the largest community colleges in the state of Ohio.

I retired July 3, 2017, as the Director of Learning Design Solutions, from the business arm of one of the largest and most prestigious college's in Northeast Ohio.

My brother said he was never so proud of me until he attended my retirement celebration and heard the wonderful sentiments expressed by the executive leaders.

The executive leaders acknowledged my accomplishments as well as recognized my value, contributions, and the legacy I left with the organization.

The words from one of the senior executive leaders left my brother's jaw dropping on the floor when he said he didn't want me to retire, even if he had to change his voice to sound like God, so that he can say, "Hugh, this is God, don't go". My brother's words filled my heart when he said how proud he was of me.

In addition, he loved the wonderful accolades the executives expressed!

Chapter One

Hugh's Leadership *Hughisms*

- ✓ I'm here for you
- ✓ Help me understand
- ✓ Let me get my arms around this...
- ✓ That's good stuff...
- ✓ WOW!
- ✓ Awesome!
- ✓ Coachable Teachable moment!
- ✓ Value Added
- ✓ I'm *glass half-full* Hugh
- ✓ It's a new day!
- ✓ Paradigm shift...
- ✓ Circle of influence
- ✓ Let me cherry pick this topic
- ✓ I am going to do a 30K foot look at this...
- ✓ What are your thoughts?
- ✓ Can we dialogue?

- ✓ This is a safe environment...
- ✓ What goes on in Vegas stays in Vegas
- ✓ I like that...
- ✓ Feedback not criticism
- ✓ What feedback do you have?
- ✓ What questions do you have?
- ✓ Moving forward...
- ✓ I submit to you!
- ✓ Thank you for that...
- ✓ Are we good ... yes... no?
- ✓ Thank you for sharing...
- ✓ Clear concise and succinct.
- ✓ That's powerful!
- ✓ Who would like to share first?
- ✓ I'm thinking out loud...
- ✓ Moving on...
- ✓ That's huge...
- ✓ Effective Communication is when the message is received as intended!
- ✓ *Yes!*
- ✓ Coachable, Teachable, Moment!

All of the "Hughisms" focus on establishing your own unique verbiage and leadership language. Most people will identify your language with your leadership communication style.

Your communication style also affords others to relate to you in a way that signals connectivity. People gravitate to familiarity and find comfort in predictability. We are "predictable" creatures by nature.

Your unique language creates a relatable culture promoting cultural relatability, as a Hughism.

In addition, your words must express your personal stamp identifying you as the author! Your "uniqueness". It is your verbal signature exclusive to only you.

Additionally, great leaders are consistently clear, concise, and succinct with their words. Exceptional leadership understand the definition of "effective communication" that it is "only when the message is received as intended".

You see effective communication is likened to a game of tennis. The volley is back and forth. There is a sender and a receiver. When you are the sender or the speaker; the other person is the receiver and/or the listener.

There is a great opportunity for you to sever the relationship if you grab the ball or you interrupt the other person by stopping them as they are expressing/sharing their thoughts and ideas, by stating to the other person, "I know what you are about to say."

Thereby not allowing them to finish and/or complete their thoughts and ideas. Unless you are physic or clairvoyant; remember people need to express their full thoughts and ideas. In other words, people need to be heard!

In fact, the character of a highly professional individual is only when you can articulate your thoughts and ideas. Successful leaders have mastered the "art of communication" by being able to "sell their thoughts and ideas".

Hugh calls this, effective communications!

Chapter Two

Communicating Effectively for Results

I believe that Effective Communication is "when the message is received as intended."

When the message is received as intended, there is a process to ensuring the message was received as intended.

Asking a question or questions is one of the recommended ways and you can't go wrong because there is only two ways to do so. You can confirm the "Message has been received as intended" by first asking, Open ended questions and Closed ended questions; Open ended question have prefix of: What, When, Where, Why and How whereas Closed ended questions have prefix of the following: Should, Will and Did.

I have a leadership philosophy of a paradigm shift which moves us from the mindset of "Traditional" verses "Non-traditional" leadership. And with this paradigm you do not have to wait until January 1st, to shift or change your way of thinking.

I also believe that this paradigm shift opens up a new way of communication which allows leaders to shift from telling, and/or saying "do as I say", which often comes across as "do as I say, not do as do."

It affords the opportunity for "Giving and Receiving "Constructive Feedback" verses the traditional dialogue of "Giving and Receiving Constructive Criticism." Which is the oxymoron of "to build you up just to tear you down."

Additionally, the art of "Giving and Receiving Constructive Feedback" will afford you the opportunity to be clear with respect of your "expectations."

In addition, you must always deliver your message so that you are clear, concise and succinct, and that there is no ambiguity and/or confusion in your message.

You must never confuse your audience with your message! It is essential that you "know" your audience! As a leader you must have your thoughts/ideas clear in your head, so that when you speak and begin to deliver your message, it comes out of your mouth exactly as intended.

Remember, being an effective communicator means that people "trust" what you are saying and your words matter. There is a high-level of accountability integrated and woven into your words. You must understand that if people can't trust you, then your words have no meaning, which ultimately mean you have no connection with your audience. *Therefore the message will not be received as intended.*

You must be able to "connect" with your audience to achieve the intended results and expectations, to be considered an effective leader as well as an effective communicator.

Here is my mantra for effective leadership communication:

Never let them see you sweat! This goes back to if you are truthful with people you will never sweat trying to think or should I say rethink about what lie I said to them the first time.

You see a leader can sometimes find themselves wanting to not tell the whole truth. Communicators, or effective communicators are comfortable speaking or presenting their message because they are sharing their truth! At least their truth in their minds-eye! And/or their truth as they believe it to be true!

Therefore, the manner that an effective leader deliver's the message to be received as intended is with authenticity, ownership, and ease. You will never see that leader sweat!

As a two-time Best Keynote Speaker and Facilitator award winner of the Cleveland Business Connect Magazine for Northeast Ohio, I learned to own the message in a manner that I believe every word I am speaking is the truth as I know it in my mind's eye!

Chapter Three

Coaching like a Leader

As a Certified Registered Corporate Business Coach (WABC), when I talk to leaders about Coaching I emphasize the point that Coaching is not about "Telling", coaching is about "asking". Asking questions to get to the heart of the issue or matter; it is the essence of coaching. You will have to remember that if a person is not ready to be coached, coaching will and can't happen.

There is a process for coaching.

Here are some steps:

1. Set the stage by creating an environment whereas the person understands you are there for them...they will trust you.
2. Open with a positive intent.
3. Understand the situation or goal to be discussed.
4. Agree on the situation or goal.
5. Acknowledge a plan of action following a brainstorming opportunity and seek alternatives.
6. Select the appropriate resolution for the best solution process and outcome.

7. Revisit an action plan for successful collaboration and continued dialogue.

I often say to leaders, coaching is not about "telling", coaching is about "Asking Questions."

You will have to ultimately get to the "Heart" of the issue. Coaching should afford a person the opportunity to get to their own destination, come to their on resolve and solve their own problems. Your goal should be to listen, teach, inspire, guide and if needed direct the person to their end goal or issue.

The metaphor for "Coaching like a Leader" is to always afford people the opportunity to steer their own "car". You are never to grab the wheel. Never become an enabler. And most importantly never become a backseat driver in the car.

Again, you are to find out what is the "motivation" of the person. Everyone has their own "motivation".

Remember, you are to inspire others. You can't motivate anyone. People must determine their own motivation. Motivation is an inner perspective for people. Your responsibility is to create an environment that will afford individuals to feel motivated, feel inspired.

People must feel as though they can show-up and bring their whole self to the job.

Motivation is the difference between you and me.

The metaphor I use for leaders to understand their responsibility when coaching is to think about a car.

The car metaphor plants a seed in the mind of most leaders that seem to make the most sense and differentiates coaching from mentoring.

Here is the metaphor:

Imagine you on a road that leads to your destination. However, on each side of the road is an endless cliff. The endless cliff represents a metaphor that if you aren't coaching well the person will drive off the cliff. Something any great leader never wants to see happen.

So, as you allow the person to get in the car and sit in the driver's seat, you don't want to get in the passenger seat. You do want to get into the rear seat. However, you are not to become a back-seat driver either. Your place in the car is to coach.

As soon as the person takes the wheel you begin your coaching. Remember half of the battle in coaching is getting someone to take the wheel.

Coaching is about asking questions to get to the heart of the issue, remember. As you begin your line of questions your goal is to get the person to the point of making their own choices and decisions.

For example, the dialogue may sound like this:

"Hugh if you go too far to the left, what do you think will happen?"

Hugh should say, "If I go too far to the left I am going to drive off the cliff."

"So, Hugh what do you need to do?"

Remember, it's all about the art of asking questions in order to get to the heart of the matter or issue.

Again, the dialogue should go like this:

"You are getting too close to the right side of the cliff. So, Hugh what do you think you should do?"

Hugh should respond by saying, "I need to get back over to the middle of the road."

Ideally, you want the person you are coaching to begin to steer their own car and come to their own resolve and solve their own problem.

You see if you grab the wheel you will cause an accident and/or create an enabling situation.

On the next page, I will share more thoughts surrounding coaching.

Traditional Management Coaching

The Leader has:

- ✓ Authority and power
- ✓ Most of the significant information (often shared only on a "need-to-know" basis)
- ✓ Final responsibility for results

Non-Traditional Coaching

The Leader:

- ✓ Focuses on obtaining your employee's buy-in to performance vs. wielding authority
- ✓ Shares information freely vs sharing it on a "need to know" basis
- ✓ Facilitates decisions vs making shared decisions
- ✓ Assists employees in defining their work vs defining the work solely on their own
- ✓ Inspires employees vs. directing and telling
- ✓ Shares the responsibility for creative solutions to problems

The heart of coaching is a relationship that a leader builds with his/her employees in order to:

✓ Increase their people's own ability to create the desired future
✓ Ask their people to examine their thinking behind what they are doing so it is consistent with the goals of the leader and the organization
✓ Being there for you, asking questions, listening, and providing helpful feedback and guidance

Some Models To Remember

Accountability shows itself in an organization when, leaders and employees deliver what they promise and committed.

✓ Goals and plans are executed on time and meets expectations
✓ When disappointments, excuses are replaced with an examination of what occurred and turned into "lessons learned" for the future, rather than a blame game; they look for the "why"
✓ High performance is the only thing that matters

Accountability shows itself in leaders and employees when:

✓ People take personal accountability for their impact on others and each other, for the success of all.

✓ People focus their attention on what they can do, regardless of what others do, however, they help everyone get to where they need to be.

✓ People take action, instead of waiting for others to act; they promote the purpose of getting everyone across the finish line.

✓ People choose to be "owners" of everything they do; thus ensuring their high level of accountability.

✓ Again, high performance is the only thing that matters.

Leaders have a choice of how and when to coach, here are some examples:

✓ In the moment Coaching
✓ All together Coaching
✓ Coaching for Expectations

In The Moment Coaching

Feedback for redirecting or acknowledgement of a high performance can happen every day and at any time. This is still a type of coaching. In the moment Coaching can result in significant benefits by acknowledging an individual's high performance and strengths for ongoing improvement. It is effective in keeping people focused on continuously sharpening their saw, which is their mind and body. It is the idea of "catching others doing something right" and letting them know it in the moment.

All Together Coaching

All together Coaching can be done in-person or by webinar. It provides an opportunity for groupings to gain the collective experience from the coach and their peers. It helps build a sense of teamwork and reinforces important business goals and objectives.

The focus of "All together Coaching" should be on successful achievements of organizational advancement holistically. All together Coaching works well when sharing best practices and strategies that ultimately achieves the results and outcomes for the success of the organization.

Coaching for Expectations

This type of coaching is the sit-down conversation between a Coach and employee(s). The focus is on the most recently observed skill or behavior or desired business expectations. The focus is on what is expected for required Coaching activities and behaviors needed in order to achieve business results.

The conversation should be focused on what worked well and what could be continued for creating best practices. The goal and or objective should be to create a strategy and action plan.

Coaching like a Leader is achieved through the tools, techniques and resources introduced in this section of the book.

My "Coaching Story" Real-talk!

In my classroom as I facilitated a leadership session in one of Ohio's leading community colleges, I met a person that opened a new door in my leadership coaching endeavors.

At one of the breaks in the session, one of my participants approached me with a question. The question was, "do you do this outside of the college?" My response was that I will have someone contact you and provide you with the process for engaging you with an independent company program.

To my surprise this was not at all what the person was asking. She shared with me that her husband was a Pastor of a church and she wanted me to help him become a better leader.

She arranged a meeting for the three of us to meet at a local coffee establishment where as I met the Pastor, and he shared his story with me. *You see we all have a story.*

The Pastor laid out his story and the net of this yielded the following needs and/or requirement of me:

✓ I don't have a college degree and need you to help me with your knowledge, skills, and resources as an educator to get to where I need to be.

✓ I have a new forming church with people I want to place in leadership positions and responsibilities and I don't know how to get them to where they need to be.

✓ I need to develop my church's mission and vision statement, and I don't know where to begin.

✓ My sermons are God inspired, however I need help structuring the presentation of my message to be received as intended.

✓ Where and how to begin and get there, was the question?

I had never ever taken up the challenge of coaching a person in the ministry, nor had I ever accepted such an awesome level of accountability and responsibility; but I did!

The mission of engaging in this type of leadership coaching spoke to my heart! It truly spoke to my heart as for the four-year experience I was never formerly compensated financially; however, I received a blessing beyond my wildest expectations.

So, I addressed each need independently and sometimes concurrently. As a seasoned facilitator of Project Management, I never used any strategic methodology and/or any of my professional learned systems in my approach. For whatever reason I started on this road, which later was a new chapter and journey in my life with a spiritual mind-set.

First, established rapport with the Pastor! We gained a level of trust almost immediately. I believed this journey was sanctioned by God!

The Pastor accepted every recommendation for learning method, resource and educational recommendation I suggested and provided.

Pastor excelled almost in an accelerated manner as if he were a sponge!

Secondly, I met with all the individuals Pastor selected for emerging leadership positions within the church.

I discovered dedicated, committed and educationally diverse individuals with a love for God!

My coaching sessions to get everyone to where they needed to be were extensive, but not tiring. I know that the months in hindsight felt like days and the time always went by too quickly.

Thirdly, developing a mission and vision statement for the church was one of the easiest I had ever done. The reason for this was because I knew that the Pastor and his leadership team believed and owned the message to be received as intended. In addition, they owned their truth; the love of God. So, it was comfortable expressing the "Why".

My experience crafting mission and vision statements for fortune 100 through fortune 500 organizations afforded me the opportunity to successfully support them with the development of their mission and vision statements for the church.

The church is now moving toward their eight-year anniversary holding true to their mission and vision statement I supported with developing.

Fourth, as a lecturer, presenter, professional trainer and two-time award winner of the Cleveland Business Connect Magazine' Best Corporate Speaker allowed me the expertise to assist Pastor with crafting structured sermons that also reduced the length significantly, so that the message was clear, concise and succinct.

Again, the Pastor received the word from God. Therefore, the message was already anointed by God. As preachers of the word of God, it is perfectly fine to ensure that the message is effective.

Even the bible states in scripture, about how we should effectively communicate!

Wisdom is the principal thing;
therefore get wisdom: and with all thy getting
get understanding.
Proverbs 4:7

Wherefore, my beloved brethren,
let every man be swift to hear, slow to speak,
slow to wrath.
James 1:19

You see I relate these two scriptures from the bible in the context of effective leadership as well.

Whether it is coaching or having a conversation with an employee or peer it is important that a leader never, ever jump to conclusions. Again, the art of listening is another one of the newest leadership imperatives. "Two ears and one

Mouth," is my mantra for leaders to remember listen more and speak less!

The ability to collect the information prior to speaking and/or providing feedback will most assuredly yield you a better "understanding".

In addition, great leadership is when you are swift to listen and slow to speak as well as never seek to intimidate or punish individuals without complete comprehension of all issues concerned.

Additionally, leaders can-not-not make time to hear their employees and include an open mind as well as the willingness to seek truth.

The results of my journey as the Pastor finalized, crystalized, and identified during my journey with this "Devine" connection was, "Iron sharpens Iron!"

In addition, I committed to years of accountability not only to the building of the spiritual Kingdom of God, but also to the physical brick and mortar aspect to the Kingdom building process.

I would leave work headed to a building that the Pastor acquired from the city to build his church. I spent countless hours, days and nights supporting the Pastor and his vision of a church.

Community and door-to-door evangelizing, praying and walking the neighborhood streets in every type of weather, as I grew in to a new creature.

It was during this process that I received my calling to preach the word of God!

As I was fighting the call, Pastor explained it was a fight I would not win. Again, Pastor explained Iron-Sharpens-Iron and I just needed to submit to the "will" of God.

My first sermon was preached in the church I helped build being witnessed by the same Pastor I supported with his journey, the leadership I supported to get to where they needed to be and honoring the mission and vision statement I helped craft as I now own the word to be delivered and received as intended.

I was ordained as Reverend, Hubert J. Littleton on August 1, 2013, in Faith Temple Church, Cleveland, Ohio, by Bishop John W. Thompson, Elder Paul Carrington, Elder Jonathan S. Pressley, and Pastor Willie J. McCreary.

The three anointed men of God, whom I call my spiritual Father's, or better my Daddy's, are Bishop John W. Thompson, Faith Temple Church in Cleveland, Ohio, Elder Paul Carrington, Senior, Pastor, Love Center

Interdenominational Church, Cleveland, Ohio, and, Pastor Willie J. McCreary, Greater Tabernacle Church, Cleveland, Ohio.

In addition, my spiritual journey also included religious and spiritual guidance from Reverend James Smith, Faith Temple Church, Cleveland, Ohio. Reverend James Smith became my moral compass reminding me to always remain holy in spite of any stone thrown my way, I should never forget I am a "Man of God".

Rev. Smith shaped me into the minister I am today who can deliver the spiritual message of God in a manner that will be received as intended.

Thank you, Rev. James Smith, for being the 'Man of God' you are and for helping me be the 'Man of God' that I am.

In addition, I can never forget the love and guidance from my spiritual mother, 'Reverend Agnes Langford", Reverend James Smith's mother.

So, as you have read, I have also been the recipient of extraordinary coaching!

I am thrilled that this chapter in my life I am proclaimed the *guru* of leadership training and facilitation. I am instrumental in a coaching process that has visibility and sustainability to this date and time!

So, coaching is not just for the professional arena it is also for the spiritual arena! If you have participants that have the "will" to be coached, they are then coachable!

Chapter Four

Conflict Resolution Leadership Style

Let's provide context regarding a definition of what is conflict.

Conflict means different things to different people. Let's review what this really means. For some, a definition of conflict involves confrontation, opposing positions, strong emotions and high-stakes differences and so on. For others, it may be a difference in opinion, perspective or personality.

One person may feel they are in a conflict situation, when the other person feels that they are just discussing opposing views. It may depend on our personal "view" of the situation.

As leaders, we need to be aware of how conflict arises and how to manage conflict. If unhealthy conflict can escalate and the spin off effects can result in lasting damage to relationships and the organization.

Conflict normally involves opposing views on one or more of the following:

✓ Relationships
✓ Territory
✓ Principles
✓ Position
✓ An uneven distribution of workload
✓ Unequal treatment
✓ Personality differences
✓ A lack of recognition

Now let's focus on how we manage conflict. Leaders will need to know the techniques for managing conflict and master the tools and skills for conflict resolution. We will consider these as methods for resolving conflict.

There are five conflict modes:

✓ Evade
✓ Negotiation
✓ Partnering
✓ Contest
✓ Adapt

All five are within us however we know one is more dominant in our communication and behavior style.

I will share my thoughts regarding the conflict style differences with respect to the methods we choose to use for managing conflict situations.

Evade:

Focusing on Your Perspective, not the other person

Evade is viewed as an assertive and uncooperative method by some people. When using this method, a person pursues his/her own concerns and will not likely have concern for others. This is an accountable method which demonstrates ownership for the situation at hand. You as the accountable person will take the position of responsibility for what is right and appropriate in the situation and not to win. Evade means "standing up for your rights", defending a position which you believe is correct without engaging in other opinions.

How to Apply:

✓ When immediate, decisive action is crucial – e.g. emergencies
✓ Important matters where unpopular methods and/or action need implementing – e.g. supporting unpopular policies, insisting on a situation requiring immediate action is critical.

✓ Issues critical to the individual or the organization you know are the right things to do.

Negotiation:

Focusing on the Other Person's Perspective, while still willing to hold on to your values

Negotiation is unassertive and cooperative – the opposite of Evading. When Negotiating an individual may neglect his/her own concerns to satisfy the concerns of the other person; there is an element of self-sacrifice in this method. Negotiating might take the form of selflessness; however, the intent is to work things out without losing too much. Yet your desire is to discover the other person's point of view.

How to Apply:

✓ You realize that you are wrong – to afford a better method to be understood, to hear other points of perspectives, and to demonstrate your willingness for resolve.
✓ The situation is extremely critical to the other person, more than to you.
✓ You want to show the other person that you will take the high-road.

Partnering:

Seeking the best outcome without rushing to judgement

Partnering is unassertive and cooperative. You don't rush to pursue your own concerns or those of the other person. Sometimes you may not immediately address the conflict. Partnering might appear to be a strategic form of diplomacy. Whereas you are seeking the best outcome without rushing to judgement, but seeking the truth.

How to Apply:

✓ Seek a mutual outcome when the potential damage of confronting a conflict outweighs the benefits of coming to the best resolution.
✓ When collecting data is important to ensuring you have the facts prior to rushing to judgement.
✓ When hearing other perspectives will afford the opportunity to resolve conflict more effectively.

Contest:

Everyone has an opportunity, if you have the ability

Contest can be considered both assertiveness and cooperativeness. The goal is to afford everyone an opportunity to flex their position with the situation. Sometimes one will give more than the other based on the weight of the situation and the value. Contest may mean splitting the difference or seeking the best alternative.

How to Apply:

✓ Positions are moderately important, but not worth the effort of dismissing and or disrupting the relationship based on the ability to reconcile.
✓ When your opponent has equal power, and is strongly committed to perceived mutually exclusive goals – for example, labor-management bargaining or getting a bill passed in Congress.
✓ When you desire a temporary settlement to a difficult situation.

Adapt:

Both parties will seek to empathize with the other

Adapt is both assertive and cooperative. Adapting involves an effort to work with the other person to discover mutual solutions which fully satisfies the concerns of both parties. It means digging into an issue to identify the underlying concerns of the two individuals and finding an alternative which addresses both sets of concerns. Adapting is the ultimate form of empathy one to the other.

How to Apply:

✓ When you want to reach a mutual resolution whereas both parties concerns are equally important.

✓ When you want to garner the perspective from others with different outlooks to come to a mutual agreement.

✓ You desire to maintain the relationship and work through a difficult situation for mutual satisfaction.

Metaphorically speaking conflict is likened to an Iceberg! (See Figure 1: Conflict Resolution Iceberg)

Often you may be able to see the conflict in action. However, you never really know exactly when the conflict started. It is a situation beneath the iceberg water line.

15% of the tip of the iceberg is considered above the waterline and is only what others see of you. It is called the business face of the individual.

In other words, the business level. 85% of who the individual and/or person is beneath the water line of the iceberg. The 85% of who the person is beneath the water line is considered the person's values, belief, thoughts and what the person stands for.

Conflict begins beneath the water line when someone's values, beliefs, thoughts and/or what they stand for is violated and/or disrespected in some way.

The emotions surrounding the situation causing the disruption of either the value, belief, thoughts, and/or what the person stands for is disrespected, is where the conflict begins. Then the conflict/emotions begin to bubble up to the top beyond the surface of the water line and into the 15% business level.

Within the 15% business level at face value is when the conflict is noted and noticed because it is now manifested usually in a public forum.

The visible part of the iceberg is very small compared to what lies underneath, much like our behaviors are like a tip of the iceberg in comparison to what lies underneath in the form of beliefs, attitudes, and experiences.

The tools, techniques and skills provided in this chapter are to manage the emotional disruption of conflict.

Leaders, remember conflict is never going to end. There is no magic wand to make everything go away or the conflict disappear.

You can only manage you and not the conflict, simply because conflict is between humans. As long as humans have feelings, which we do, you can never ever tell anyone how they should feel; simply because they have that human right.

Otherwise the moment you tell someone they can't or shouldn't feel a certain way, rest assured you now have entered into a world of conflict!

So, we offer these tools and techniques to minimize, mitigate and/or eliminate conflict.

Figure 1 Conflict Resolution Iceberg

Chapter Five

Change that is Impactful

Let's begin with context surrounding change!

"Change refers to the ability of an organization to improve the design and implementation of initiatives and to reduce cycle time in all organizational activities."[4]

"Anytime a change is made in an organization, it has the underlying purpose of improving the way the organization is functioning. In simpler terms, to increase productivity of a unit, group, or an organization is the primary basis for change."[5]

"One meaning of "managing change" refers to the making of changes in a planned and managed or systematic fashion. The aim is to more effectively implement new methods and systems in an ongoing organization. The changes to be managed lie within and are controlled by the organization.

Perhaps the most familiar instance of this kind of change is the change or version control aspect of information system development projects. However, these internal changes might have been triggered by events originating outside the organization, in what is usually termed "the environment."

Hence, the second meaning of managing change, namely, the response to changes over which the organization exercises little or no control (e.g., legislation, social and political upheaval, the actions of competitors, shifting economic tides and currents, and so on). Researchers and practitioners alike typically distinguish between a knee-jerk or reactive response and an anticipative or proactive response."[6]

A leader will need to have the following tools in their toolkit regarding change!

"Change refers to the ability of an organization to improve the design and implementation of initiatives and to reduce cycle time in all organizational activities."[4]

"Anytime a change is made in an organization, it has the underlying purpose of improving the way the organization is functioning. In simpler terms, to increase productivity of a unit, group, or an organization is the primary basis for change."[5]

"One meaning of "managing change" refers to the making of changes in a planned and managed or systematic fashion. The aim is to more effectively implement new methods and systems in an ongoing organization. The changes to be managed lie within and are controlled by the organization. Perhaps the most familiar instance of this kind of change is the change or version control aspect of information system development projects. However, these internal changes might have been triggered by events originating outside the organization, in what is usually termed "the environment." Hence, the second meaning of managing change, namely, the response to changes over which the organization exercises little or no control (e.g., legislation, social and political upheaval, the actions of competitors, shifting economic tides and currents, and so on). Researchers and practitioners alike typically distinguish between a knee-jerk or reactive response and an anticipative or proactive response."[6]

I recommend Kotter's Eight Steps Change Management System[1] to leaders for their toolkit!

"Kotters Eight Steps of Change"

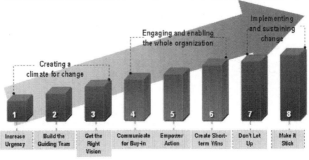

*Kotter, John P. and Cohen, Dan S. The Heart of Change. Boston: Harvard Business School Press

Figure 2 Kotters Eight Steps of Change

Let's review Kotter's defined 8 step processes:[1]

1. Establish a sense of urgency

– Examine market and competitive realities.

– Identify and discuss crises, potential crises or opportunities.

– Create the catalyst for change.

2. Form a powerful coalition

– Assemble a group with enough power to lead the change effort.

– Develop strategies for achieving that vision.

3. Create a Vision

– Create a vision to help direct the change effort.

– Develop strategies for achieving that vision.

4. Communicating the Vision

– Using every channel and vehicle of communication possible to communicate the new vision and strategies.

– The guiding coalition teaching new behaviors and leading by example.

5. Empowering others to act on the vision

– Removing obstacles to change.

– Changing systems or structures that seriously undermine the vision.

– Encouraging risk taking and non-traditional ideas, activities and actions.

6. Planning for and creating short term wins

– Planning for visible performance improvement

– Recognizing and rewarding employees involved in these improvements.

7. Consolidating improvements and producing still more change

– Using increased credibility to change systems, structures and policies that don't fit the vision.

– Hiring, promoting, and developing employees who can implement the vision.

– Reinvigorating the processes with new projects, themes and change agents.

8. Institutionalizing new approaches

– Creating the connections between new behaviors and corporate successes. – Developing channels to ensure Leadership development and succession.

In addition, I have my own roadmap and process that describes change both personally and professionally.

Change has an extraordinary process that consist of the following steps:

- ☐ Step one: Shock
- ☐ Step two: Anger
- ☐ Step Three: Resistance
- ☐ Step Four: Buy-in
- ☐ Step Five: Action Plan

Then there is the internal process which is the change you must make within yourself to move through the change process.

Let's review:

Step One: Shock

Shock is usually when someone is introduced to a new process, method, procedure, and/or expectations unexpected.

A person can remain in a state of shock for 15 minutes or 15 years. Unfortunately, if a person doesn't get over a shock state of a situation within 15 minutes or a reasonable amount of time and they become stuck, they potentially can be on hold in that state of mind for 15 years.

I suggest leaders go home stew over the situation, get over it overnight and get up the next morning, go back to work and get into the game!

Step Two: Anger

Anger occurs when a person holds onto the change situation past 24 to 48 hours. This becomes a cycle of inner turmoil. The individual is stewing over the change situation continuously. This can last 15 minutes to 15 years.

Step Three: Resistance

When an individual moves into the resistance phase of a change situation, they have made a conscience decision to bolt themselves down and they are making a public statement, *"they shall not be moved"*.

Leaders must be observant of people in the mode of resistance to change. Resisters to change very often can revert to sabotage. The resistance phase is one of uncertainty, so they must be vigilant in their leadership role.

Step Four: Buy-in

Buy-in is seeking total collaboration from the person and/or team. This is when you want people to come to agreement with your/organization's goals, mission, objective and most importantly the vision.

Getting buy-in demands that people trust you. Remember, trust is doing what you say, saying what you mean and most importantly, the caveat is that you must follow through.

When you have accomplished trust with your team, department, and organization, the art of getting buy-in is second nature.

Step Five: Action Plan

Developing an Action Plan is a must do. You must ensure there is follow-up after the work is put-in.

So, what is an action plan?

A sequence of steps that must be taken, or activities that must be performed well, for a strategy to succeed. An action plan has three major elements:

(1) Specific tasks: what will be done and by whom.

(2) Time horizon: when will it be done.

(3) Resource allocation: what specific funds are available for specific activities.

Great leaders will always ensure there is an action plan in place!

Chapter Six

The Golden Rule for Successful Leadership

The Golden Rule (not to be confused with Golden Law, Golden ratio, or Golden act) is defined in many ways, here is one:

For other uses of the term, please see Golden Rule (disambiguation)[3]

The **Golden Rule** (can be considered as a **law of reciprocity** in some religions) is the principle of treating others as one would wish to be treated. It is a maxim of altruism seen in many human religions and human cultures.[1][2]

The maxim may appear as either a positive or negative injunction governing conduct:

- One should treat others as one would like others to treat oneself (positive or directive form).[1]
- One should not treat others in ways that one would not like to be treated (negative or prohibitive form).[1]
- What you wish upon others, you wish upon yourself (empathic or responsive form).[1]

The Golden Rule differs from the maxim of reciprocity captured in do ut des—"I give so that you will give in return"—and is rather a unilateral moral commitment to the well-being of the other without the expectation of anything in return.[3]

The concept occurs in some form in nearly every religion[4][5] and ethical tradition.[6] It can also be explained from the perspectives of psychology, philosophy, sociology, human evolution, and economics. Psychologically, it involves a person empathizing with others. Philosophically, it involves a person perceiving their neighbor also as "I" or "self".[7]Sociologically, 'love your neighbor as yourself' is applicable between individuals, between groups, and also between individuals and groups. In evolution, "reciprocal altruism", is seen as a distinctive advance in the capacity of human groups to survive and reproduce, as their exceptional brains demanded exceptionally long child-hoods and on-going provision and protection even beyond that of the immediate family.[8] In economics, Richard Swift, referring to ideas from David Graeber, suggests that "without some kind of reciprocity society would no longer be able to exist."[9]

All this simply means is "One size fits all" which is that if you like to be yelled at why shouldn't I? So, someone may say "You talking to me, You talking to Me?"

Some people don't like being yelled at, period.

Another way to look at the Golden Rule is:

If you like vanilla ice cream, you may serve only vanilla ice cream at your party.

However, 75% of your guests may not like vanilla ice cream and only 25% of people like vanilla ice cream.

Will you be OK with that? I think not. Here is another way to look at the Golden Rule:

75% of the people you come in contact with you have difficulty with and 25% of the people you come in contact with are utilizing the Golden Rule philosophy. Would you be pleased with that? Again, I think not.

There is another philosophy I am recommending to progressive leaders for building relationships with their teams and organizations.

I am recommending leaders learn to "Meet people where they are!" to get them to where they need to be!

Meeting people where they are is not the Golden Rule. There is nothing within the philosophy of the Golden Rule that afford you the opportunity to meet people where they are. Or treat people the way they want to be treated.

Meeting people where they are offers the opportunity to discover how the other person wants to be treated and then understand, empathize, and determine the other person's wants and needs.

Communication is the only way to get to the level of meeting people where they are.

One other thing to note:

Leaders will need to add "Purpose" to the formula of extraordinary leadership for legacy building! Purpose will also provide individuals with the need to seek the "Why" when it comes to helping employees embrace the concept of their value and the value of their body of work.

Leaders will want to challenge the idea of purpose so that employees have a keen sense of self-worth to add sustenance to their desire to be a part of the organization. When companies/organizations invest in their employees and give them a sense of belonging it manifests into retention within the organization.

In addition, remember leaders there are at least five generations in the workplace today!

You will want to discover their "Why" and influence their purpose for value-added performance.

I believe that in order to meet the generational mix leaders will need to realize what I consider the "needle-in-the-haystack".

In simple terms the "needle-in-the-haystack" is the "Ex-factor" for the individuals. What is their driver? What is the inner motivation? What is also, the value-proposition of the individual? It is their purpose!

Once again, meeting people where they are is the key that will unlock all of those doors.

Allow me to give you one other point that will build a legacy for an extraordinary leader. A leader who is "Discerning".

Discerning leaders are perceptive, judicious, astute, discriminating, and selective regarding his/her words, actions, and process.

This leader clearly understands good from bad and has the capability to relate it to his/her team in a non-disruptive manner, ensuring success and high-performance.

Extraordinary discerning leaders have the uncanny ability to "see what is coming".

I believe my recommendations are sustainable for extraordinary leadership success when building a legacy!

Chapter Seven

Managing My time to help the Team be On-Time

Time management is really a misnomer!

You may think you manage your time in reality this is rarely the case.

More often, time manages you!

I want to introduce leaders to managing time this way simply because most leaders are constantly telling their teams/organizations they must manage time. It is a misnomer! People can only manage themselves, not time.

Time is the "new compensation"!

In addition, if we agree that there are only 24 hours in the day. What will happen if we give people one more hour making it 25 hours in a one day. What do you think the average person will do with the extra hour? The answer is, sleep! Most will sleep with the extra hour. Most will not be more productive, efficient, or effective.

With that said, we must urge people to begin managing themselves.

Here is the paradigm:

- ✓ Leaders will need to analyze what is in your control and begin to control it.
- ✓ Leaders will need to realize what are the crucial and essential goals and expectations
- ✓ Leaders will need to establish a paradigm shift within their organizations emphasizing within their organization people need to get things done when they need to be done.

In addition, the strategy is to create action plans.

Suggested planning!

It is recommended that every minute of planning will save you ten-minutes in execution. We offer the 80/20 rule where as if you have ten things to do on your list of priorities, if you accomplish 2 of those most important things you have successfully achieved critical portion of your day. 20% of your activities will account for 80% of your results.

In addition, there is the 90/10 rule. If you accomplish one important thing on your list of ten you have achieved the bulk of your crucial work. The other nine things can be reassigned

Managing Yourself Require the following steps:

✓ **Decisions** – decide on what you must do first; use task list, checklist.
✓ **Discipline** – commit to doing what you said you are going to do! Hold yourself and others accountable to be responsible, therefore owning everything you do.
✓ **Determination** – completion is the order of progressive individuals and organizations. Perseverance and seeing things through to its finish and following the process is what creates great leaders.

Followed by these elements:

- ✓ **Planning** – establish a roadmap for the journey and follow the process.
- ✓ **Prioritization** – decide what will be done first, based on your 80/20.
- ✓ **Preparation** – create a sense of urgency and readiness for what needs to be accomplished.
- ✓ **Procrastination** – don't rush to action; always be calculating, measured and methodical

Leading by example will afford others to see that it can be done. Whatever "it" is, if others see you can do it, they will believe they can do it, as well.

Leaders, remember managing your time and getting your team to manage their time is to always set clear and defined expectations.

Change your language! Yes, change your language! Instead of saying "as soon as possible" say "I will need this at 3:00pm". No longer will you say "I need this by close of the business day". You will say "I need this at 5:00 pm". Based on your time zone!

Additionally, making the priority list is critical! Develop your list the night before! A checklist will increase your output by 25% the first day.

Also, learn to adapt a method to touch task and/or assignments one-time. It will potentially increase your productivity 50%

Finally, setting clear and defined expectations will create and foster good habits and benchmarks for others to follow.

All of my thoughts in this chapter will support leaders to manage their own time and help others to be on-time!

Chapter Eight

Leading Beyond Yourself, bringing others along with You

Leading beyond yourself, and bringing others along with you is the ultimate art of leadership.

If you want to lead beyond yourself you must move yourself out of the way! I have found in my 25 plus years in a leadership role and managing people at every level, that this chapter will provide you with the tools, skills, and techniques to lead others beyond yourself.

In addition, coaching, guiding, training, facilitating and designing/developing leadership curriculum, that there are leaders who truly believe they are the center of the universe. Not true!

Leaders, great leaders realize that they are to inspire others to get to where they need to be. That is, allowing others to rise to their full potential of leadership.

Great leaders are those who recognize they are to afford other voices, thinking and ideas to come before their voice.

People need to know that they are being heard. People need to know that their ideas are being recognized. People need to know that they have a part and most importantly, a significant part in the process.

Bringing others along with you, is getting them to trust you enough to want to follow or better yet go along with you and 'reflect' you!

Remember leaders, you must not categorize everyone the same.

It is important to keep in mind and in the forefront that people are individuals and will need to be brought in to the fold in a unique manner with the focus being when they are ready.

That will mean that leaders will be required to know their audience! Leaders need to be accountable to those whom they are responsible for and too.

Accountable to the point of always observing and knowing what makes them tick.

What motivates them, and how they may continue to meet them where they are. Meeting people where they are will always be the principle leadership characteristic that will set you apart.

Chapter Nine

Emotional Intelligence for Leadership

I must first provide a definition for emotional intelligence. Emotional Intelligence is defined as a set of competencies demonstrating the ability one has to recognize his or her behaviors, moods, and impulses, and to manage them according to the situation.

Emotional Intelligence is not about being agreeable, kind, pleasant, polite, considerate, courteous, sympathetic, cordial, warmhearted, proper, refined, genteel, and/or acceptable.

So, leaders don't get it twisted!

Emotional Intelligence is about being trustworthy, direct, measured, purposeful and most importantly, truthful.

Leaders, emotional intelligence is not about being touchy feely!

Emotional Intelligence is about being acutely aware of the feelings of others. There again, not tip toeing around others watching out that you are always politically correct. It is about being highly in-tuned with words, your actions and the process that may impact others regarding their performance, delivery and execution, when it comes to their feelings.

Emotional Intelligence is not about being overly emotional, poignant, affectionate, exciting, and/or excitable, passionate, and/or expressive.

It is about being keen, unflustered, imperturbable, composed, levelheaded, and most importantly, smart with your emotions.

The net results for leaders and their leadership with respect to mastering emotional intelligence is as a tool in their tool kit is the following:

It will benefit them both personally and professionally. Personally, better health, whereas they will be less likely to be high-jacked emotionally, increased optimism and confidence. When it comes to professionalism, 85% of people have greater career success with increased levels of emotional intelligence.

Emotional Intelligence affords leaders the ability to reason well in difficult situations. It will give them leverage when it comes to problem solving, less workplace conflict and effective communication.

The bottom-line, win-win for leaders, is to understand the following five phrases with regards to emotional intelligence[9]:

Always have a line of sight of self-awareness; know who you are.

Self-regulations; control your emotions.

Self-motivation; always remember you can only inspire others and can never motivate anyone.

Empathy; always try to meet people where they are, having an understanding for everything and everyone.

Most importantly, always always keep in the forefront the idea of building sustainable relationships that are beyond just rapport!

Chapter Ten

Essentials for First-Time Leaders

What is "Leadership Style"?

A leadership style is a leader's method of providing direction, implementing plans, and inspiring people.

Essentials for First-Time Leadership Success

- ✓ Recognize five leadership imperatives you need to lead
- ✓ Identify three characteristics that successful leaders have
- ✓ Describe ten leadership competencies needed to lead a successful team

Five Leadership Imperatives

- ✓ Effective Communication
- ✓ Trust
- ✓ Commitment
- ✓ Process
- ✓ Results

Effective Communication

When the message is received as intended.

Effective Communication

- ✓ Ensure the message is received as intended to achieve full commitment and **acknowledgement of connectivity**
- ✓ Know when to move to a **crucial conversation**
- ✓ Effective communicators <u>minimize</u> **conflict, confusion/ambiguity** when **setting expectations**

Effective Communication

- ✓ Great leaders recognize they **must meet people where they are**; promoting **diversity in thought**
- ✓ Effective leadership is when you clearly understand your team's diverse **communication** and **behavior styles**
- ✓ Understand the difference in providing "constructive criticism" versus **"constructive feedback"**

Effective Communication

- ✓ Leaders, remember you can never over communicate!

Trust

- ✓ "Doing what you say, saying what you mean and following through."
- ✓ **Trust**
- ✓ Build a foundation of trust, be an *authentic* leader
- ✓ Inspire trustworthy behavior amongst the team/ *Take greater initiative/ Try new ideas/ promote accountability*
- ✓ Create a *fear-free* environment/ Foster an environment affording others to *ask for help*

Commitment

"Having the **"Will"** to do!"

Process

Refers to the way leaders identify a problem, develop solutions, analyze data, or reach agreement.

Following the process:

- ✓ Get things done
- ✓ Complete tasks
- ✓ Identify problems
- ✓ Develop sustainable solutions
- ✓ Analyzing data
- ✓ Ensure agreement is reached
- ✓ Meeting goals
- ✓ Planning and organize

Results

What is leadership oriented results?

Trust, Credibility, Respect, and Accountability

Results

- ✓ Develop a **clear focus**/ Focused on **short** and **long-term goals** --- **Practice Stephen Covey's Quadrant 2-Focus**
- ✓ Develop/ Create a **culture** focused on **accomplishing goals** with a purpose for **achieving objectives**
- ✓ Strive to achieve **critical initiatives** with the **end-in-mind**

Results

Bottom-line...

"Effective leadership promotes a culture of **trusting** the process."

Three Primary Characteristics Of Successful Leaders:

Diagnose

Coach

Reinforce

Leadership Characteristics

1. Diagnose

Monitor performance/**Diagnose non-performance and high-performance**

2. Coach

Ask questions that drive to the heart of the issue/**Facilitate decision making and planning to achieve results...build relationships**

3. Reinforce

Reinforce actions and conditions that support high performance/**Manage personal and practical needs**

Ten Leadership Competencies

First, we need to acknowledge the *"Four Stages for Success"* ...

Stage 1:

Form a clear vision-the general shape of what success looks like

Stage 2:

Ensure everyone's agenda is heard and explored

Stage 3:

Skillfully discuss issues involved---deepen the understanding of goals and surface any hidden agendas

Stage 4:

Ensure commitment and buy-in at all levels of leadership

Ten Leadership Competencies

(1) Define a very clear picture of the future, *a vision for the team*

(2) Be authentic - *even if it means being vulnerable*

(3) Ask questions – *"Appreciative Inquiry" process*

(4) Talk about difficult topics --- *you may get the knot in the stomach*

(5) Follow through on commitments – *you cannot, not have time*

(6) Let others share their ideas and thoughts – *even when they do not align with yours*

(7) Listen, Listen, Listen... *two ears --- one mouth!*

(8) Address non-performing players – *even the ones you really like*

(9) Have fun, but never at others' expense – *respect for the individual at all times*

(10) Be confident, dependable and *accountable*

Whenever you think about these essentials for leadership new or seasoned, just remember the most important essential is being authentic! Leadership is when you know who you are and why you are in the position of leadership.

The roadmap for leadership is endless, so just keep building and adding on to the road. Even better, give the road your name!

The journey is one you must create for others as well as for yourself! Great leaders ensure that the journey is exciting, productive, engaging, memorable, enriching enhancing and most of all inspirational!

Chapter Elven

Leading with the Courage to say No, and Walk Away

This is a chapter most people would suggest is telling them how to get fired! Often when I coached people on this topic they would most often ask, "wont this get me fired?"

The answer is no!

Leading with the courage to say No, and Walk Away is simply having the courage to ask for help. Yes, asking for help. You see most people have a fear of asking for help when the following occurs.

I don't know how to do something, when you expect me too. Or, I don't have the answer to something, and you believe I should. And/or I need more information to deliver on something and I am too afraid to say so.

Fear is a debilitating thing. Courage is facing all of those fears. Courage is asking for help! And not fearing the consequences of judgement.

Leading with courage is letting others know that you don't know everything and that's why you ask for help. Again, you see asking a question is a sign of great leadership as well. Great leaders ask, ask, and then ask some more.

There are only two ways to ask a question:

✓ Open End
   o Open End: What, When, Why, How.
✓ Closed End
   o Closed End: Should, Will, Did.

In addition, leading with the Courage to say No, is coaching your people to ask questions, having no fear of consequences. They need to know!

So, here is the "Big" idea! The Courage to say No, is actually learning to say "When". Learning to say "When" is saying also asking for more. It is letting the other person realize and recognize that I don't have all of the information I need. Or I am not clear in my understanding of my expectations.

Never walk away without having all of the information you need to be successful. Then have the courage to walk away! When you have the courage to walk away, you know you will be successful accomplishing your expected results.

Most of my coaches expressed that they have walked away and then were not successful because of two reasons. 1. They were afraid to ask for help. 2. Because they didn't say when, therefore they didn't get all of the information required to successfully accomplish their expectations, thus failed in their assignment.

The definition of the word fear is: an unpleasant emotion caused by the belief that someone or something is dangerous, likely to cause pain, or a threat.

I'd like to share another personal experience with you! A person with a high level of authority snapped at me, and it was to my complete surprise and disappointment. As a leader and father figure to me I was stunned by the experience.

Sometimes people say what they would do in certain situations, however until it happens to you in the moment, you really don't know what you will do.

So, when this leader snapped at me it was during a situation he should have never allowed himself to be in simply because it compromised his position and stature as a leader.

Without giving full detail of the situation to further expose this leader, the point of this story is to present why leaders should remember to never afford others to place them in a position whereas they feel humiliated and/or flustered and frustrated which will cause them to act out in a manner completely out of character stunning to others.

Unfortunately, we don't express it to that person who obviously caused you to be in the situation, whereas you are behaving in a fashion that is inappropriate. it's always the person who is unaware of what is to come, who walks right in the line of fire and gets shot down like a deer in headlights, asking what just happened. They are at the right place but the wrong time. *That would be me!*

This person played the victim so that this leader would feel sorry for him and empathize incorrectly. Yes, I said "empathize" incorrectly. Which means you put yourself in the place of the wrong person, because you were being manipulated. *Yes, you were being used...*

As you know I promote "empathy" in great leaders as the new paradigm shift. However, this not the acceptable way to demonstrate empathy.

Sometimes, even the most astute leaders never see it coming and are hit so hard it blindsides them, making them unaware of the manipulation, and/or sense that they are being used. This form of blindsided is known in the leadership world as 'unconscious bias'.

Now, on the other hand, there are those leaders that "Know it" and allow it for whatever reason! Regretful; we don't have time in this book to analyze this theory.

Nevertheless, this leader lost a great deal of respect from me!

That one isolated and unfortunate incident, potentially destroyed a trusted relationship and rapport, that took years to build. *In an instant it was potentially destroyed.*

Leaders, this passage is for you to realize that you must be responsible for your word, your actions and the process. Never compromise your own values for the satisfaction of others. Be true to you and know your own truth in any given situation. *It is your responsibility!*

Leaders have the propensity to present a wall of fear. Most often it is because they are not approachable. Or not willing to express any level of vulnerability. Letting others into their space of meeting people where they are.

As well as affording others the ability to show their susceptibility.

Leaders remember, you don't have to know everything and neither does anyone else! And it is OK to be vulnerable.

So, always have the Courage to say "No" and "Walk Away".

Chapter Twelve

Recognizing Who I am and being You!

Who are you? Branding is huge when it comes to recognizing who you are and really being you. *Living your truth!*

So, what is a brand? Your brand is recognizably the way people identify you. It is your trade mark. In many ways it becomes your personality. The traits you most frequently and often exhibit to others.

In addition, knowing who you are creates an image and awareness to others that they can have confidence in you. Others will trust you for being consistent and self-aware.

Without saying, sometimes people will respect you just because you know who you are. That is not arrogance, its confidence and that is why people follow a leader.

Two specific things that will afford others to follow you are: Trust and Confidence.

Again, trust is defined by Hugh Littleton as "doing what you say, saying what you mean and most importantly follow-through." Secondly, it is confidence. If people don't trust you they definitely will not have confidence in you and so they will not follow you.

All of this boils down to recognizing who you are. Other school of thought is that you must know your value. Having a value-proposition is a must have for leadership. I am not referring to just knowing your value, which is what everyone needs to know and understand.

I am advocating knowing your self-worth! Never compromising your belief in what is responsibly the right thing to do.

Allow me to stand on the word value for a moment.

Please, please, please know your value, your self-worth. There are people who will try to diminish your value in a heart-beat just to make themselves look better; more important; bigger and special. While trying to make you less important; smaller and non-distinct.

You must be "set-a-part", unique and sometimes exceptional!

So, getting back to value proposition, it is the message you have that speaks to who you are and how you plan to show-up.

You see, you must show-up and bring your whole-self to the job every day. In other words, bring your intellect, your passion, your skills, and knowledge to the table.

Know that when you are peculiar, and that is not a bad thing! It just means that you are uncommon. Who wants to be considered "cookie-cutter". Know that to be set-apart is a *good-thing!*

When you are comfortable in your own skin and can resist being afraid of what others may say or think, *then you will find it easy to be you!*

When you are able to be you, now as a leader you can concentrate on building a legacy of extraordinary leaders and leadership!

About the Author

 Hubert J. Littleton, President of *Hugh Littleton Consulting, LLC,* (HJL Leadership Solutions), has experience in manufacturing, customer service, service industries, financial organizations, non-profit, government agencies and healthcare sectors. He is well versed in supervisory, management, C-suite, and leadership skill development solutions.

Hugh has been very instrumental in implementing many continuous improvement initiatives with companies ranging from small manufacturing to Fortune 500 companies; providing training across the US and abroad internationally.

Experience

Hugh has over 20 years facilitation/training and learning solutions experience as a leadership expert in the soft-skills and quality programs arena. Recognized nationally for leading organizations through the process of cultural transformation and organizational development solutions.

Hugh has afforded his leadership expertise to many premiere organizations such as Lincoln Electric, Alcoa, Forest City Enterprises Inc., Rockwell Automation Inc., Greater Cleveland Regional Transit Authority, Global Corporate College, Cuyahoga Metropolitan Housing Authority, Cleveland Metropolitan School District, The Smithers Group, Inc., Forest City Enterprise, Cuyahoga Community College, Corporate College, University Hospitals, Cleveland Clinic Hospitals, as well as other corporate Supervisory, Management, C-Suite, and culturally diverse audiences.

Background

Hugh has provided leadership development to more than 25 organizations in Northeast Ohio, across the United States, and in the United Kingdom.

In addition, as an ISO/QS9000 Registered Lead Assessor, RAB, Certified, Hugh has assisted in the implementation of organizations project management achieving ISO/QS9000 certification. Additionally, he is a WABC, Certified Register Corporate Coach and Certified Program Planner.

About the Author

The result of outstanding contribution to his profession, Hugh recently was named the Keynote Speaker of the Year for 2014, through the Cleveland Business Connect Magazine.

In addition, Hugh was the winner of the 2010 CBC, Cleveland Business Connect Magazine, Best Speaker and Facilitator Award. Hugh was the 2016 finalist for CBC's Keynote Speaker of the Year.

Testimonials

Mr. Littleton is by far one of the finest trainer/facilitators that I have worked with in nearly 20 years. His depth of reaching and impacting audiences spans from front-line workers to the C-Suite executives in many of Northeast Ohio's corporations and community agencies. Mr. Littleton has not only been requested by the internal departments at Cuyahoga Community College, where he worked for many years, but by scores of senior-level executives who were adamant about him being the only person allowed to train their teams. Mr. Littleton is an effective trainer and facilitator across all professional development areas as well as an experienced executive coach who offers leadership coaching to many senior-level company executives. In retirement, Mr. Littleton will be able to focus full-time to impacting leadership teams through his private consulting firm, HJL Leadership Solutions.

Dr. Linda D. Woodard, CWDP, GCDF

One-Stop Operator ⊕ Experienced Community College Workforce Development Administrator & Career Dev. Professional

Testimonials

If I had the ability to establish a training organization, Hugh Littleton would be at the top of my list! Hugh is a consummate professional. He is able to design a session that is engaging while tailoring the message for the audience. Hugh is particularly skilled at engaging disparate viewpoints. He always manages to bring a smile to every work environment and helps you to see the silver lining.

Dr. Monique Umphrey

VP Workforce Innovation & Dean - IT Center of Excellence at Cuyahoga Community College

My name is Michael Polovick and I am currently retired from The Smithers Group. Prior to January 1 of this year I served as the Vice President of Human Resources for the company.

I am writing this letter as a reference for Hugh Littleton.

As background, The Smithers Group is a team of companies diverse in the technologies employed. All of

Testimonials

the companies have a common mission of providing high quality science based services to clients. A privately held company, Smithers has been successful for more than 90 years and has grown considerably during this time. The company now has operations on 3 continents with more than 800 employees. This level of success is attributed to the shared values and culture of the company.

As Smithers continued to grow, steps were taken to ensure that the company did not compromise on its values or culture. Knowing that one cannot just "hope" to sustain these key success factors, there has been considerable effort put forth to ensure that the key success drivers are shared with all new employees and their managers. Smithers sought partners that understood the company's values and culture, believed in them as well, and could convey them as passionately and credibly as Smithers management does.

I want to let you know that one such partnership was with Hugh Littleton. Hugh has done a great deal to assist in developing Smithers leaders. The company is fortunate in having a long-term relationship with Hugh as coach/trainer

Testimonials

for "Smithers University". The program involved training employees from all company's locations for future leadership roles.

I was personally involved in leading the process for the last 10 years. And the one consistent feedback that I received was how much everyone appreciated Hugh's contributions to the program. His communication skills are such that he could cross cultural boundaries whether the individual was from Switzerland, England, Germany, China or the US. Hugh has the ability to engage everyone throughout the process... even those who would prefer to sit on the sideline and not get involved. And he has the ability to make the process interesting and challenging such that participants look forward to the day's activities.

Today we live in a highly critical society where it is rare to get high praise from one individual let alone several. The fact is, that in my ten years with Smithers and Smithers University, I had never heard a negative word about Hugh. Instead, each year Hugh's evaluations showed very positive feedback.

Testimonials

Hugh is an exemplary leader in motivating, training and facilitation.

Sincerely,

Michael Polovick

Vice President of Human Resources (Retired)

The Smithers Group

Testimonials

Hugh and I first worked together in his capacity as lead trainer for Cuyahoga Community College (Tri-C). Hugh demonstrated an advanced understanding of coaching, training and development. He is the rare trainer with the ability to connect with those with barely a high school diploma to providing training for executive leadership teams.

Hugh has an amazing depth and breadth of experiences that allow him to be in the moment during training sessions affording him the opportunity to nuance the training to better connect with those in the room. Hugh brings expert knowledge of training and development, training modalities, and the ability to work with internal and external stakeholders.

For Tri-C's corporate clients, Hugh's expertise was the difference in building sustainable relationships with the college's corporate training clients.

Albert Lewis, Jr.

VP of Economic & Workforce Development

Photos

Photo 1 Warrensville Heights Area Chamber of Commerce (WHACC) Breakfast Series

Photo 2 Judging Channel 5 ABC Academic Challenge

Photo 3 Author in the UK, The Smithers Group Inc. - Rapra

Photo 4 Author with former NBA Chicago Bulls, Mayor Bradley D. Sellers (Mayor's forum workshop – Cuyahoga Community College, Tri-C)

Photo 5 Author's parents, Rev. Roosevelt Littleton and Margaret V. Littleton

Photo 6 Author speaking at a Warrensville Heights Area Chamber of Commerce (WHACC) event.

Photo 7 Author speaking at (CMHA) Cleveland Metropolotian Housing Authority leadership forum

Photo 8 Author at Corporate College Nascar leadership team building event

Photo 9 Author in the UK, The Smithers Group Inc. - Pira

Photo 10 Author with his brother, John A. Littleton

Photo 11 Author moderating at Mayor's Workforce at Cuyahoga Community College, Tri-C

Photo 12 Author conducting a 7 day leadership workshop for Smithers Group - UK

Photo 13 Author at his Retirement Recognition Ceremony with College President Alex Johnson, Cuyahoga Community College

Notes

Referenced Work

[1]Kotters Eight Steps of Change

[2]Thomas Kilmann-Instrument

[3]Golden Rule, Wikipedia, the free encyclopedia

[4]Dave Ulrich, Human Resource Champions, 1997

[5]Glen Varney, ASTD T&D Handbook, 4th edition, 1996

[6]Fred Nickols, Change Management 101: A Primer, 2004, home.att.net/~nickols/change.htm

[7]Glen Varney, ASTD T&D Handbook, 4th edition, 1996

[8]Fred Nickols, Change Management 101: A Primer, 2004, home.att.net/~nickols/change.htm

[9]Daniel Goleman, Author Emotional Intelligence,1995

www.hjlleadershipsolutions.com

contact@hjlleadershipsolutions.com

Butterfly Typeface Publishing

the **Butterfly** Typeface

Contact us for all your

publishing & writing needs!

Iris M Williams

PO Box 56193

Little Rock AR 72215

www.butterflytypeface.com